Contents

The colour blue

All of these are blue.

Which would you choose to make a blue picture?

Vic Parker

Heinemann

Powys

Little Nippers

H www.heinemann.co.uk/library
Visit our website to find out more information about **Heinemann Library** books.

To order:
☎ Phone 44 (0) 1865 888066
📄 Send a fax to 44 (0) 1865 314091
💻 Visit the Heinemann bookshop at www.heinemann.co.uk/library to browse our catalogue and order online.

First published in Great Britain by Heinemann Library, Halley Court, Jordan Hill, Oxford OX2 8EJ, part of Harcourt Education.
Heinemann is a registered trademark of Harcourt Education Ltd.

Editorial: Jilly Attwood and Claire Throp
Design: Jo Hinton-Malivoire and Tipani Design (www.tipani.co.uk)
Models made by: Jo Brooker
Picture Research: Rosie Garai and Sally Smith
Production: Séverine Ribierre

Originated by Dot Gradations
Printed and bound in China by South China Printing Company

ISBN 0 431 17340 0 (hardback)
08 07 06 05 04
10 9 8 7 6 5 4 3 2 1

ISBN 0 431 17345 1 (paperback)
08 07 06 05 04
10 9 8 7 6 5 4 3 2 1

British Library Cataloguing in Publication Data
Parker, Vic
Mixing Colours with Blue
752
A full catalogue record for this book is available from the British Library.

Acknowledgements
The publishers would like to thank Trevor Clifford for permission to reproduce the photographs in this book.

Cover photograph reproduced with permission of Trevor Clifford.

The publishers would like to thank Annie Davy for her assistance in the preparation of this book.

Every effort has been made to contact copyright holders of any material reproduced in this book. Any omissions will be rectified in subsequent printings if notice is given to the publishers.

The paper used to print this book comes from sustainable resources.

What can you think of that is blue?

blue
beads

blue
car

blue
gloves

Blue and red

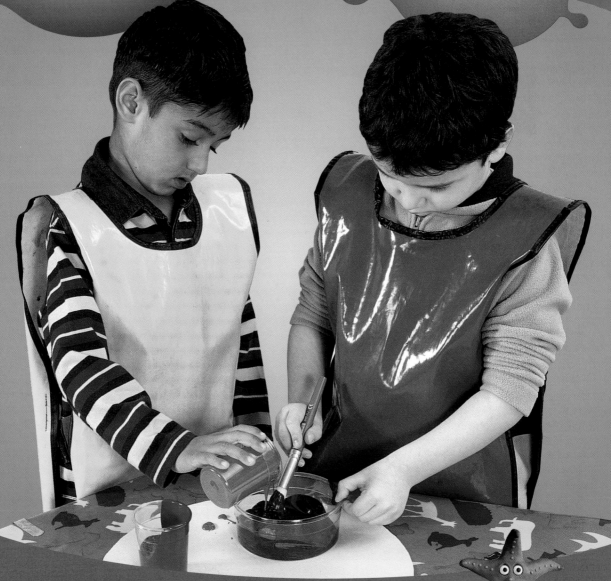

Blue is **cool**. Red is **hot**.

Mix them together and what have you got?

purple!

Indigo

A **lot** of blue and a little bit of red makes ...

inky indigo.

Violet

A **lot** of red and a little bit of blue makes ...

vivid violet.

13

Blue and yellow

Blue like the **sky**.

Yellow like
butter.

Green

Mixing blue and yellow makes ...

a green **butterfly**.

Blue and green

Add gleaming green
to true blue to make ...

peacock-bright turquoise.

Blue and black

Black makes blue go

darker...
darker...
darker...

until it becomes the **navy blue** of the night sky.

Count the shades

Cars come in lots of different shades of blue.

cyan

sapphire

azure

royal

midnight

Index

The end

Notes for adults

The *Mixing Colours* series explores what happens when you blend two colours (occasionally three) together. The books focus on the mixing of pure paint colours, while also leading children to think about other pigments, such as crayons, chalks, pens and dyes. There are four titles in the series, focusing on the primary colours and white. Used together, the books will help enable children to differentiate between colours and begin to understand how they are made. They can also be used to encourage children to talk about what happens when colours are mixed, using appropriate language such as lighter, darker and shade. The following Early Learning Goals are relevant to this series:
Creative development
Early learning goals for exploring media and materials:
• explore what happens when they mix colours
• understand that different media can be combined.

This book encourages young children to think about varying shades of blue and which ones they might use to draw or paint blue items. It will inspire them to explore what happens when they mix blue with other colours, and invite them to experiment with the resulting different colours to make paintings, drawings, collages, constructions, masks and models, etc. The book will help children extend their vocabulary, as they will hear new words such as *indigo* and *violet*.

Follow-up activities
• See how many blue objects your child can find around the house, and compare the shades. You might like to explore words like pale, dark, bright, sky blue, turquoise, etc.
• Fold some large sheets of newspaper into four paper hats. Mix blue paint with other colours to make purple (or indigo or violet), green, turquoise and navy blue. Paint each paper hat a different shade, then decorate by sticking on bright sweet wrappers, sequins, feathers, etc.
• Mix blue paint with other colours to make purple (or indigo or violet), green, turquoise and navy blue. Use the paint to decorate some plain eggcups with bright patterns.